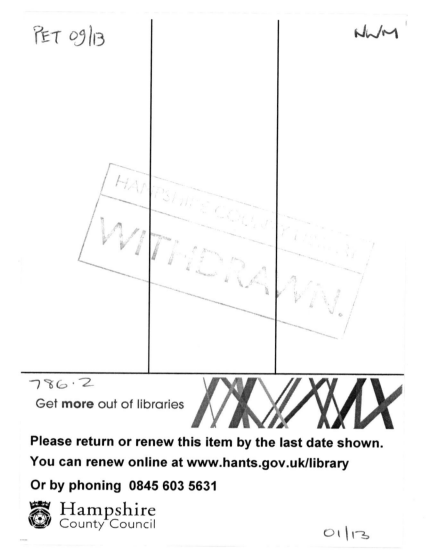

Strictly Dance

21 ballroom hits for keyboard

Strictly Dance

21 ballroom hits for keyboard

© 2012 by Faber Music Ltd
First published by Faber Music Ltd in 2012
Bloomsbury House 74–77 Great Russell Street London WC1B 3DA
Edited by Lucy Holliday
Music arranged and processed by Chris Hussey
Photograph © Thinkstock
Printed in England by Caligraving Ltd
All rights reserved
ISBN10: 0-571-53734-0
EAN13: 978-0-571-53734-1

ARE YOU LONESOME TONIGHT?

Words and Music by Roy Turk and Lou Handman

Suggested Registration: 12-string Guitar (or Jazz Guitar)

Rhythm: Waltz

Tempo: ♩ = 80 **Swung**

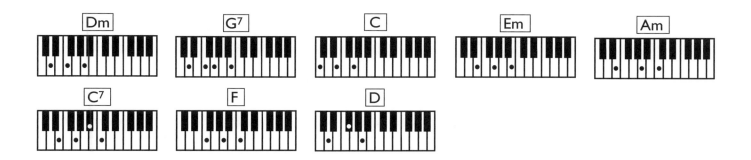

CRY ME A RIVER

Words and Music by Arthur Hamilton

Suggested Registration: Trumpet

Rhythm: Shuffle

Tempo: ♩ = 69 **Swung**

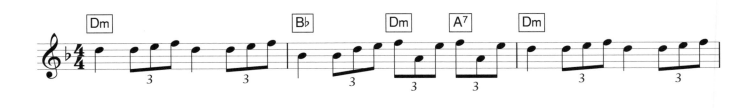

Now you say you're lone - ly,____

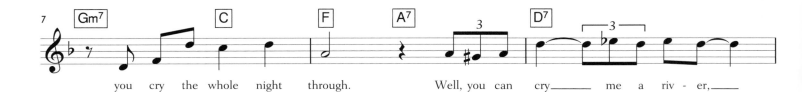

you cry the whole night through. Well, you can cry____ me a riv - er,____

cry me a riv - er,____ I cried a riv - er____ o - ver you.

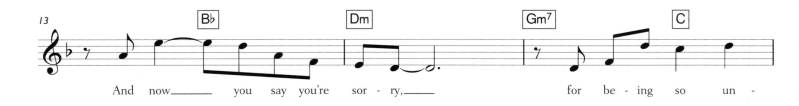

And now____ you say you're sor - ry,____ for be - ing so un -

- true. Well, you can cry____ me a riv - er,____ cry me a riv - er,____

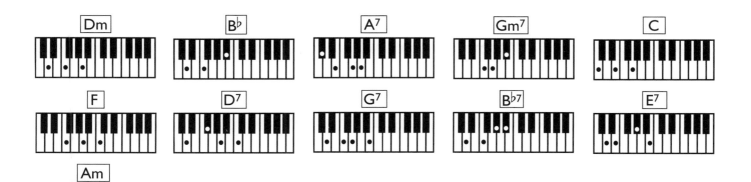

GREASED LIGHTNIN'

Words and Music by Jim Jacobs and Warren Casey

Suggested Registration: Rock Guitar

Rhythm: Surf Rock

Tempo: ♩ = 144

9

HABANERA FROM 'CARMEN'

Music by Georges Bizet

Suggested Registration: Flute

Rhythm: Habanera (or Tango)

Tempo: ♩ = 120

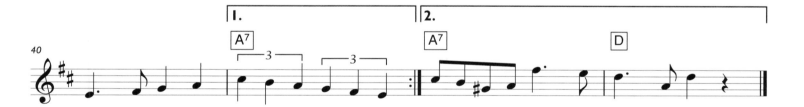

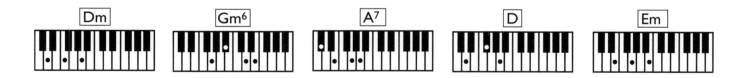

HELLO DOLLY

Words and Music by Jerry Herman

Suggested Registration: Clarinet

Rhythm: Ragtime

Tempo: ♩ = 138 Swung

Hel - lo Dol - ly, well, hel - lo

Dol - ly, it's so nice to have you back where you be -

- long. You're look - ing swell - Dol - ly, I can

tell, Dol - ly, you're still glow - ing, you're still

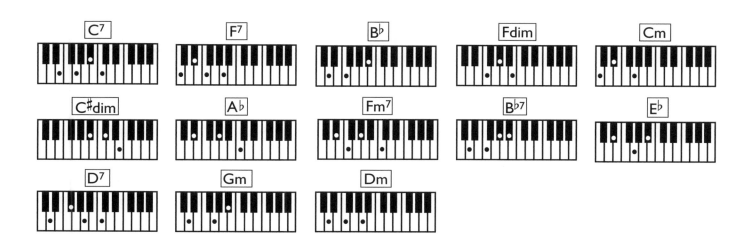

HE'S THE GREATEST DANCER

Words and Music by Bernard Edwards and Nile Rodgers

Suggested Registration: Synth. Reed

Rhythm: Samba

Tempo: ♩ = 108

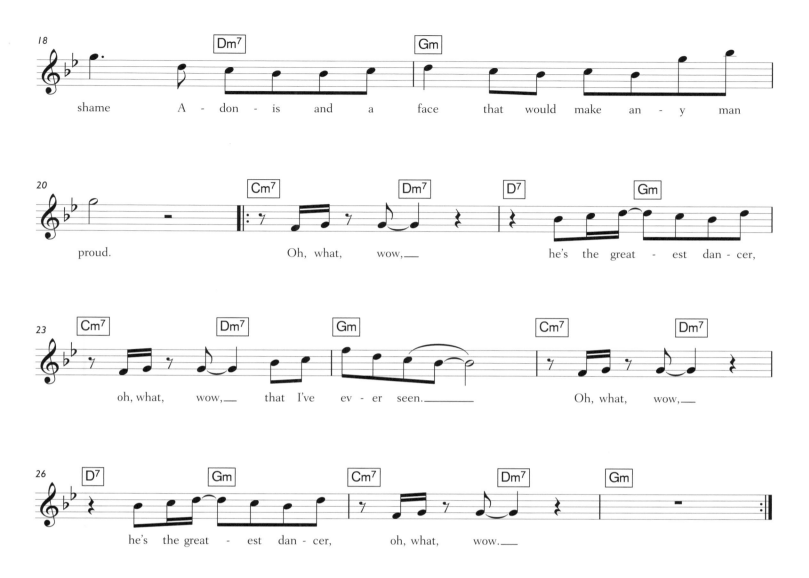

shame A - don - is and a face that would make an - y man

proud. Oh, what, wow,__ he's the great - est dan - cer,

oh, what, wow,__ that I've ev - er seen._____ Oh, what, wow,__

he's the great - est dan - cer, oh, what, wow.__

HOW CAN I BE SURE

Words and Music by Felix Cavaliere and Edward Brigati, Jr

Suggested Registration: Accordion

Rhythm: Waltz

Tempo: ♩ = 160

pit - y I can't seem to find some - one who's

as pret - ty and love - ly as you.____

How can I, how can I, how can I,____

how can I be sure? I real - ly wan - na know...____

How can I, how can I, how can I,____ I

real - ly wan - na know, real - ly wan - na know.____

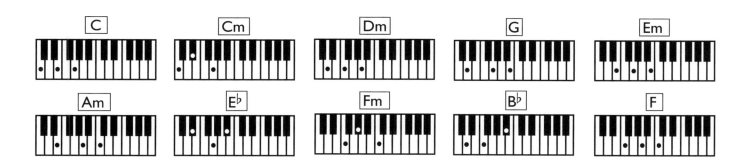

I GOT RHYTHM

Music and Lyrics by George Gershwin and Ira Gershwin

Suggested Registration: Harmonica

Rhythm: Ragtime (or Charleston)

Tempo: ♩ = 152 **Swung**

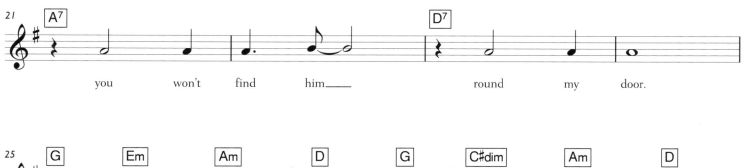

you won't find him___ round my door.

I got rhy - thm,___ I got mu - sic,___

I got my gal,___ who could ask for an - y - thing

more, who could ask for an - y - thing more?

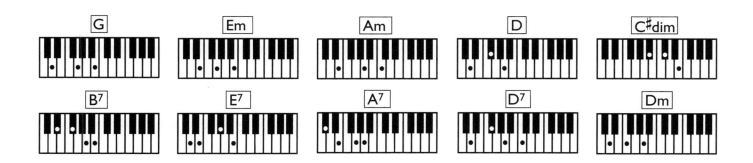

IT DON'T MEAN A THING (IF IT AIN'T GOT THAT SWING)

Music by Duke Ellington
Words by Irving Mills

Suggested Registration: Trombone

Rhythm: Swing (or Quickstep)

Tempo: ♩ = 152 **Swung**

JUMP IN THE LINE

Words and Music by Harry Belafonte, Ralph De Leon, Gabriel Oller and Steve Samuel

Suggested Registration: Steel Drum

Rhythm: Salsa

Tempo: ♩ = 160

when she dan - ces, oh broth - er, she's a hur - ri - cane in all___ kinds of weath - er.

Jump in the line, rock your bod - y in time. (O. K., I be - lieve you.)

Jump in the line, rock your bod - y in time. (O. K., I be - lieve you.)

Jump in the line, rock your bod - y in time. (O. K., I be - lieve you.)

Jump in the line, rock your bod - y in time.

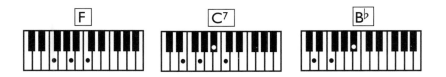

MAMBO ITALIANO

Words and Music by Bob Merrill

Suggested Registration: Marimba

Rhythm: Salsa

Tempo: ♩ = 144

MEMORY FROM 'CATS'

Music by Andrew Lloyd Webber
Text by Trevor Nunn after T S Eliot

Suggested Registration: Recorder

Rhythm: Waltz

Tempo: ♩ = 126

Ev - 'ry street lamp seems to beat_____ a fa - tal - is - - - tic warn - ing._____ Some - one mut - ters_____ and a street lamp gut - ters,_____ and soon it will be morn - ing._____

D.C. al Fine

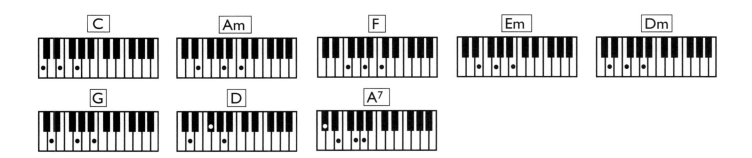

MR. BOJANGLES

Words and Music by Jerry Jeff Walker

Suggested Registration: Whistle

Rhythm: Jazz Waltz

Tempo: ♩ = 132 **Swung**

then he'd light - ly_____ touch down.____

That's Mis - ter Bo - jan - gles,

call - ing Mis - ter Bo - jan - gles,

Mis - ter Bo - jan - gles, come back and dance, and dance, and

dance, and dance, please__ dance._____

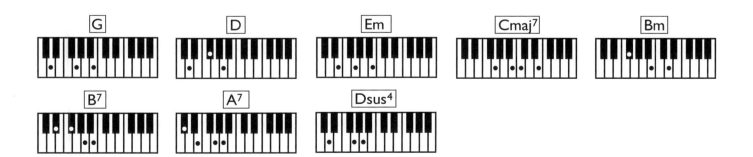

POR UNA CABEZA

Music by Carlos Gardel

Suggested Registration: Violin

Rhythm: Tango

Tempo: ♩ = 104

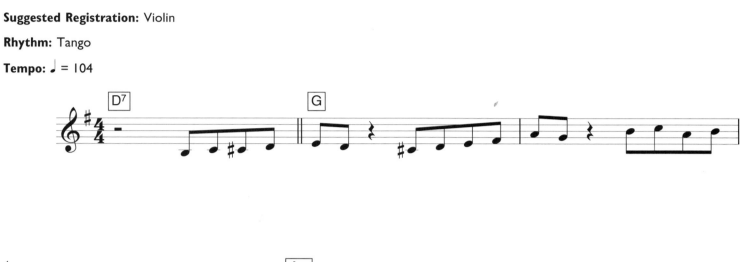

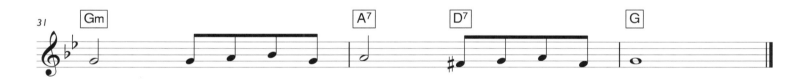

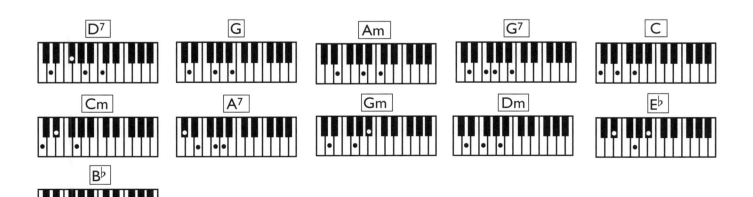

SING, SING, SING

Words and Music by Louis Prima

Suggested Registration: Piano

Rhythm: Swing (or Lindy Hop)

Tempo: ♩ = 138 **Swung**

SLEEPING BEAUTY WALTZ

Composed by Pyotr Ilyich Tchaikovsky

Suggested Registration: Strings

Rhythm: Waltz

Tempo: ♩ = 152

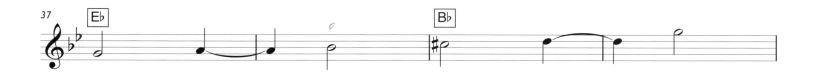

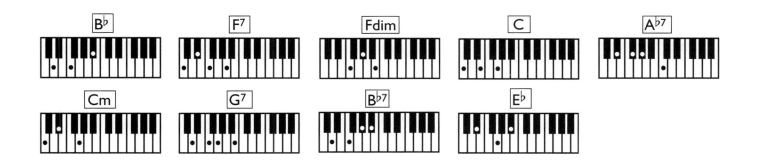

TOO DARN HOT

Words and Music by Cole Porter

Suggested Registration: Saxophone

Rhythm: Ragtime (or Quickstep)

Tempo: ♩ = 138 **Swung**

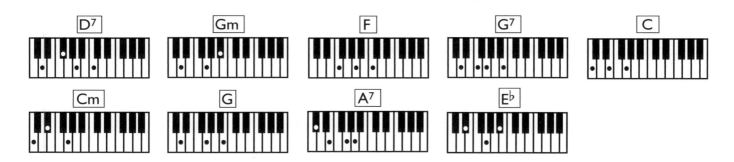

UNA MÚSICA BRUTAL

Words and Music by Eduardo Anibal Makaroff, Philippe Maurice Cohen Solal and Christoph Hermann Mueller

Suggested Registration: Accordion

Rhythm: Tango

Tempo: ♩ = 108

Des - cu - brim - os vos y yo, en el tris - te car - na - val,

u - na mú - sic - a bru - tal, mel - o - dí - as de do - lor.

Des - par - tam - os vos y yo, y - en el len - to div - a -

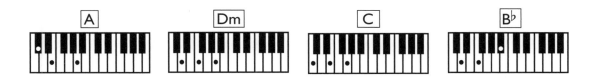

WHY DON'T YOU DO RIGHT? (GET ME SOME MONEY TOO!)

Words and Music by Joe McCoy

Suggested Registration: Clarinet

Rhythm: Swing (or Foxtrot)

Tempo: ♩ = 120 **Swung**

WISHIN' ON A STAR

Words and Music by Billie Calvin

Suggested Registration: Acoustic Guitar

Rhythm: Rumba

Tempo: ♩ = 84

come,___ and I'm wish-ing on all___ the lov-ing we've___ ev-er done. I'm

wish-ing on a star,_____ to fol-low where you are.___

I'm wish-ing on a star,_____ and I wish on all___ the

rain-bows___ that I see. I'm wish-ing on a star._____

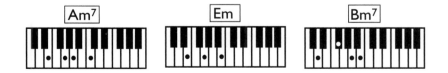

YOU CAN'T STOP THE BEAT FROM 'HAIRSPRAY'

Music by Marc Shaiman
Lyrics by Marc Shaiman and Scott Wittman

Suggested Registration: Rock Organ

Rhythm: Surf Rock (or Jive)

Tempo: ♩ = 152

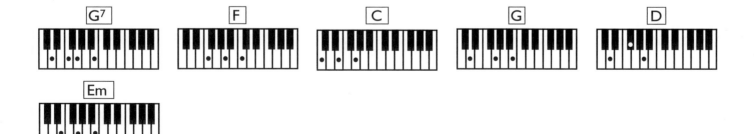

The Easy Keyboard Library

An expansive series of over 50 titles!

Each song features melody line, vocals, chord displays, suggested registrations and rhythm settings.

*"For each title ALL the chords (both 3 finger and 4 finger) used
are shown in the correct position – which makes a change!"*
Organ & Keyboard Cavalcade

Each song appears on two facing pages,
eliminating the need to turn the page during performance.

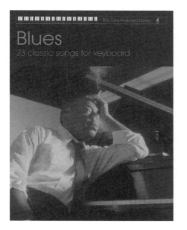
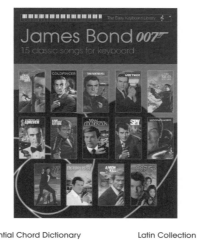

The 00s	The Essential Chord Dictionary	Latin Collection	The Seventies
Big Band Hits	Favourite Hymns	Love Songs Vol 1	Shirley Bassey
Billy Joel	The Fifties	Love Songs Vol 2	Showtunes Vol 1
Blues	Film Classics	Motown Classics	The Sixties
Broadway	The Forties	Movies	Soft Rock Collection
Celebration Songs	Frank Sinatra	Music Hall	Soul Classics
Christmas Carols	George & Ira Gershwin	Nat King Cole	Strictly Dance
Christmas Songs	George Michael	The Nineties	The Thirties
Classic Hits Vol 1	Gilbert & Sullivan	No.1 Hits Vol 1	Traditional Irish Favourites
Classic Hits Vol 2	Glenn Miller	No.1 Hits Vol 2	TV Themes
Cliff Richard	Great Songwriters	Popular Classics	The Twenties
Cole Porter	I Try & 10 More Chart Hits	Pub Singalong Collection	Wartime Collection
Country Songs	Instrumental Classics	Queen	West End Hits
Disco	James Bond	Rock 'n' Roll Classics	Whitney Houston
The Eighties	Jazz Classics	Scott Joplin	

To buy Faber Music publications or to find out about the full range of titles available
please contact your local music retailer or Faber Music sales enquiries:

Faber Music Ltd, Burnt Mill, Elizabeth Way, Harlow CM20 2HX
Tel: +44 (0) 1279 82 89 82   Fax: +44 (0) 1279 82 89 83
sales@fabermusic.com   fabermusic.com   fabermusicstore.com